VISUAL

SOCIAL MEDIA MARKETING

Harnessing Images,
Instagram, Infographics
and Pinterest to Grow
Your Business Online

by **Krista Neher**

#VSMM

Visual Social Media Marketing

Neher

For general information on our other products and for services or technical support please see www.bootcampdigital.com or Contact Customer Care at 646-450-2267.

ISBN-10: 0983028621

Printed in the United States of America

First Edition

ACKNOWLEDGMENTS

Special Thanks To...

My mother, the most amazing woman I know, for her constant inspiration, support and strength,

Joe Busam for phenomenal design work and making my life better every single day,

Kim Quindlen for her endless revisions and for making sure this book was actually published,

Alexandria Webb for amazing editing.

KRISTA NEHER

Contents

– – – – – – – –

KRISTA NEHER

1 INTRODUCTION

First off, this book isn't about photography or how to take photos. I don't know much about taking good photos, and many would say that I have terrible design sense. This book is about how images are playing an important and growing role in your social media and internet marketing strategy and how you can take advantage of this trend.

I've been doing social media marketing since its inception, before social media was even a recognized term. Social media sites often come and go (I originally started doing MySpace marketing) and while the hot trends fade away, the one constant is people.

Social media is really just about connecting with people.

One of the trends that I've seen in the last few years in social media is that it is getting cluttered. People are overwhelmed with content. An average person on Facebook is connected to 130 people plus an additional 80 groups, events and pages. This means that there are over 200 people fighting for our attention each day. If each of those people post five times a day it adds up to over 1,000 updates in a single day - and that is just on Facebook!

People are becoming overwhelmed by social networks, trying to maintain accounts and staying up-to-date with the most recent and relevant content for them.

The more people are overwhelmed with content online, the more content curation is emerging as a trend. Social networks like Facebook and LinkedIn create algorithms to help surface the content in which people actually have an interest.

Even in the early days of the internet, this was referred to as signal vs. noise. The signal is the content and information that people truly find interesting. The noise is the other stuff that shows up in their newsfeed. As marketers trying to break through the noise, we must create signal content.

What this means is that to break through the clutter, we have to be more strategic than ever before about creating content that people want. As a business or an individual, if you want to gain attention you must create content that people want and deliver it in a format that appeals to them. Otherwise you will be filtered out with the noise.

As we start to consider the issue of overwhelming content and the challenge for businesses to create the right content in the right format, one trend shows up again and again. Images and visual content are increasingly what people want online. Visual social media marketing #VSMM is emerging as the key way to grab attention.

It makes sense that images are emerging as the way to break through the clutter. The phrase *a picture is worth a thousand words* refers to the fact that our brains can consume, process and understand more information faster through images than text. Communicating visually forces us to distil our ideas down to the key point or to communicate brand messages simply through images.

Visual content is most consumed, viewed and clicked on by social consumers today.

This book is your guide to this overwhelming trend in digital marketing. It will show why images are taking over as the preferred form of communication, as well as how to take advantage of this opportunity.

KRISTA NEHER

2 WHY VISUAL SOCIAL MEDIA MARKETING?

The Latest Trends in Social Media are Visual

The latest trends in social media, internet marketing and content marketing point to images and visual content as the content that consumers want. Consider these statistics:

- Facebook reports that images get 50% more interactions than other content.[1]
  - Over 6 billion photos are uploaded to Facebook every month.[2]
  - Photos get 7 times more likes and 10 times more shares than links.[3]
- Flipboard, the #1 application for iPad, is essentially a visual representation of content with images as the focus.[4]
- Pinterest, an image-based sharing social network, is exploding in popularity and has grown 4000% in the past 6 months. It features images to represent the

content that is Pinned or shared on the site and is the third most popular social network online.[5]

- Instagram is a leading application that allows people to take and share beautiful photos from their smartphone. It was recently acquired by Facebook for a whopping $1 billion and has over 100 million users.[6]
  - There are 575 likes and 81 comments by users every second.[7]
  - When Hurricane Sandy occurred, Instagram users snapped 1,278,925 photos.[8]
- Images are the most shared links on Twitter.[9]
- 40% of people respond better to visual information than plain text.[10]
- Publishers who use infographics grow in traffic an average of 12% more than those who don't.[11]

The data shows that consumers in social media prefer images and visual content. If you are considering the content that your customers want or the content that your customers will share, images should be at the top of your list.

The other thing that this data highlights is that images aren't just the most consumed content - they are also the most shared content. If you want to gain "viral spread" (which I prefer to call social spread) images can be your key to success since they are the most shared content online.

There is good reason for this. The reality is that we can communicate more information more quickly via images than text.

- 90% of information transmitted to the brain is visual.[12]
- Images and visual concepts are processed 60,000 times faster in the brain than text.

- 40% of people will respond better to visual information than plain text.[13]

This shows that images aren't just important; they are actually a more effective and efficient way for people to consume and understand your content and stories.

You Need an Image Strategy

The bottom line is that you need an image strategy for your business. If you want to be successful on social networks you must have a strategy to incorporate relevant and appropriate images.

Images are more than just a strategy for Instagram, Pinterest or Facebook posts (although I'll cover those in this book). The idea is that images should be at the core of your social media and internet marketing strategy. If you don't have a plan for images you'll miss out on the opportunity to connect with your audience.

As social media has become more competitive you can't afford to miss out on or ignore this opportunity. You must have a strategy for images or you won't only miss out on the opportunity to get traffic and awareness from Pinterest and Instagram, but you will also become less effective on other social networks.

An Overview of the Book

This book is your guide to creating an image strategy for your social media and internet marketing so that you can be among the first to really take advantage of this emerging trend.

In this book I will show you everything you need to be successful with images, and some easy ways to create amazing image content that gets you attention online.

The first section of the book will cover how to create an image strategy for your social media and online marketing. This is where you'll learn how to think about images as social content, as well as the types of images needed for success.

Next, I'll cover the core social media sites that revolve around images: Pinterest and Instagram. These two new social networks have tremendous growth rates and are amazing places to study the growth of the visual web and the visual content that consumers want.

Finally, I'll share the leading simple image tools that you can use to drive your business. I'll show you easy ways to create infographics, get stock photos, and tons of simple creative ideas for how to create your own images to drive your business and your brand.

I'm excited that you made the smart choice to learn about the visual web and images while it remains a leading edge strategy. By taking advantage of this early and adopting these strategies you'll be poised to get more attention than your competitors.

3 YOUR IMAGE STRATEGY FOR VISUAL SOCIAL MEDIA MARKETING #VSMM

A strategy for images isn't just about creating good images; it is about creating highly consumed and highly shared content for social media and your website. It is a strategy that goes beyond individual social networks or pieces of content. It is becoming a basic building block for success online.

The good news is that most people 1) haven't realized it yet and 2) don't know exactly what to do about it, so you still have the opportunity to get ahead.

Steps to Building an Image Strategy
Assess the Landscape
Start by assessing the image landscape at your business, in your industry and for your category. What images are out there? What images are being shared? What types of images aren't used yet? This will help you to begin to understand how you can communicate visually, as well as the gaps that exist in your current image inventory.

Assess Existing Images
The first thing to do in the assessment stage is to understand the images that exist already. This will give you a feel for the

types of images that already exist, as well as gaps in your current image strategy.

Start with a Google image search to see the images that are already indexed by search engines. Go to images.google.com and search for:

• Your company/business/organization
• Your products or services
• Your top executives or public figures
• Competitors
• Competitor products or services
• Industry terms
• Complementary product categories
• Complementary businesses/products/services

Take note of the images that are indexed by search engines. What images show up? What is missing? How does it represent your organization? How are images telling the story of your business?

Look at images on other sites as well. Do the same searches on image sharing sites to see if you get different results. Look at:

• Flickr.com (the leading photo sharing website)
• Facebook photos
• Instagram (a photo sharing and photo creating application)
• Pinterest (where pins are based off of images)

Looking at other photo sites will give you a feel for the current inventory of images. The goal of the landscape assessment is to understand:

• What photos already exist.
• How well do existing photos represent your organization.
• What your competitors are doing with images.
• Gaps in the types of images shown in search engines.

Images People Share

Content that exists and content that people like, engage with and share aren't always related. Content that is shared is often different than content that you find in searches online. If your goal is to increase your reach, awareness and footprint online with images, then sharability should be one of your top metrics. The first step is to understand the types of images that are shared.

Assess the images that are shared that relate to your business, competitors and your industry. Also take note of the types of images that are popular. Here are some ways to do this:

- What images get Pinned? Since Pinterest is such a visual site and 80% of pins are repins (which means that they are re-posted), Pinterest can be a great site to assess the sharability of a particular type of image. Go to www.pinterest.com/source/yourdomain.com to see what content is already getting pinned. Don't just look up your site, look up competitors, products/services, industry terms and associations.
- Search Pinterest for keywords related to your industry to understand the types of images that people are sharing.

- Search Instagram to see the photos that people are taking on mobile phones that are related to your business, competitors and industry.
- What images are popular on Facebook? Look at pages, profiles and groups. What images receive a lot of likes, shares and comments? What do they have in common?

A basic understanding of the current image landscape is the first step in building a strategic image strategy for your business. Spend some time exploring before jumping in.

Non-Image Content that is Popular

In addition to just looking at images, think about how you can translate other content that you have into images. For example, if you have a popular blog post on how to complete a task, could you create an image that shows the steps?

Assess the content that you currently create and share on your website, blog and through social networks. Can it be recreated visually?

At this point, take inventory of the content that your audience likes. In the last section of the book I'll show you examples of the different types of image content that you can create.

Assess Your Inventory

Once you've had the opportunity to look at the landscape, take a moment and assess your current image inventory. What kinds of images do you already have? Are they interesting and relevant? Do they in and of themselves tell a story?

Many organizations have huge libraries of images that aren't shared online (for a variety of reasons). After you begin to understand the types of images that will represent your business well, assess what you already have.

This will help you to understand what you need. We'll get into this in more detail in the upcoming section on Images and Your Website as well as Images and Social Networks. Before you start to assess your needs, take inventory.

Marketing Objectives

Once you have a handle on the types of images that exist and get shared, take a moment to consider your marketing or business objectives for images, for social media and for internet marketing overall.

While we won't go in depth into understanding your marketing strategies at this point (I have an entire chapter dedicated to this in my bestselling book The Social Media Field Guide), it is important to make sure that you understand what you want to achieve.

Specifically, images can be effective in achieving the following strategies:

- Building awareness for your business.
- Augmenting your existing strategy on Facebook, Twitter or other social networks.
- Driving traffic to your website.
- Generating interest in highly visual products.
- Improving and enhancing your overall web presence.
- Increasing shares and spread on social networks.

- Increasing conversions.
- Attaining links for SEO (search engine optimization).

Your specific goals and objectives might be different. Either way it is important to understand your primary goals upfront to help justify your effort on the back end.

Target Audience

One other key consideration is to understand your target audience. Who are you trying to reach with your content and images? It is worthwhile to pause and figure out exactly who you are trying to reach.

Once you understand your target audience and who you want to reach, it will be easier to create relevant images that your audience loves and that meet your marketing objectives.

Assess Your Needs, Create Images, Adjust and Repeat

These last steps in creating your image strategy are covered in the remainder of this book. Chapters 2 and 3 will cover how to assess the images that you may need to be successful on your website and on social networks. The last section of the book will show you the different types of images that you can create including infographics, using Instagram and how these images are shared through Pinterest. Finally we'll give you tips and tricks on creating images that are highly shared, including resources to create amazing images for your business.

4 IMAGES AND YOUR WEBSITE

There are 2 parts of your online marketing strategy that require great images. The first is to have images for your website and the second is to have images for your social media content.

Why You Need Good Images on Your Website

The answer to why you need good images on your site isn't just to make it look visually appealing. Obviously, most websites have images to communicate the brand identity and to create an aesthetically pleasing experience. However, those aren't the only reasons that images are important.

As images are shared more online and as they are the focus point of how content (even text content) is shared online, it is important for businesses to have powerful, relevant and effective images that describe their content throughout their website.

If you want your website or website content to be shared on the new visual web it must have a relevant image that describes the content visually.

A few months ago, I was looking at Pinterest to see what content had been pinned from our website. I noticed, strangely, that a picture of me was pinned and looked to see why someone was pinning my image. The actual webpage that was pinned was about our free report on Google+. The page on our website included the entire report, but there wasn't a picture to represent the report. So, when someone wanted to Pin our report to share it with their friends, they had to choose a different image from the page. Next I looked at what happened when we shared our reports on Facebook. We had the same problem. We didn't have an appropriate image for our content, so users had to choose among other photos that were not relevant to the content (like my photo).

I went back and created images to represent our free reports. This meant that if someone wanted to share on Facebook or Pin the report there was a relevant photo to represent the post. As you can see below, without a relevant image the post wasn't ideal for pinning, but once we added an image, people could share and pin our content. What we found was that we received more pins, Facebook posts and more traffic simply by adding an image.

Even on Facebook, the image of the link is highlighted, so having a relevant image can increase the click-through-rates on the links that you post. As you can see, having a relevant image makes our Facebook shares easier to read. As a side note, I took this screen shot around Halloween when my profile picture was from a Halloween costume. I do not have pink hair or fangs.

Krista Neher

In case you missed it - check out our free report on Google Plus http://bootcampdigital.com/cmo-briefing-google-for-business-report/

Business Leader Briefing: Google+ For Business Report
bootcampdigital.com
Boot Camp Digital presents our FREE report

Like · Comment · Share · Promote · 2 seconds ago ·

The bottom line is that having images on our website is key to driving social shares of our site content which ultimately drives traffic to our site.

The key takeaway is that if you want your content to be shared on the visual web, you have to have relevant images on your website for each piece of content. Even if the webpage doesn't require an image, image content is key to sharability on the new visual web.

EXAMPLE:

To bring this concept to life, look at the difference between how two similar brands are represented on Pinterest – Starbucks and a local coffee shop called Coffee Emporium (they have amazing coffee and an amazing café experience). The screenshots show content pinned from Starbucks.com and content pinned from www.coffee-emporium.com.

Starbucks

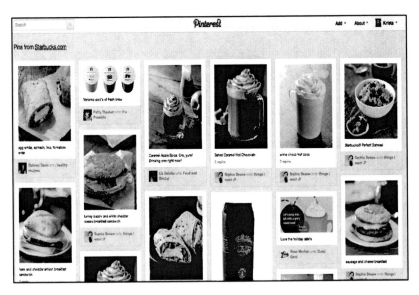

Coffee Emporium

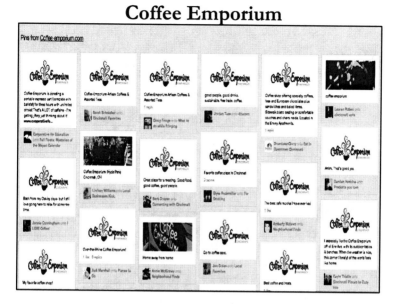

Which coffee shop do you want to go to based on the images that are shared online?

You'll notice that Starbucks has lots of appetizing photos showing their beverages – they make me want a coffee! Since Starbucks has lots of great images on their site, their site is pinned more often, and the images build brand equity and awareness for Starbucks.

Coffee Emporium on the other hand only has a handful of images on their website, primarily their logo. When their site does get pinned, the accompanying image is a boring picture of their logo (yawn). While they are still getting some traction from Pinterest they could be generating more if they had attractive and relevant photos to share.

Coffee Emporium vs. Starbucks for Sharing On Facebook

The same is true on Facebook – if I found Coffee Emporium

and wanted to share the link on Facebook there are only 3 photos found on their homepage (none of which is their logo). This limits how effectively posts involving Coffee Emporium will display on Facebook.

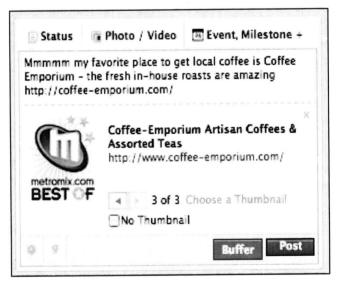

With Starbucks, my only option when sharing their homepage is their logo, however the interior pages all have relevant photos that can be used as the thumbnail when posting to Facebook, making the brand more visually appealing.

As you can see from this example, images are becoming the key to how your content is shared across the web. If you don't have good images, people are less likely to share; and when they do share, it won't garner as much attention.

How to Make Your Website Visual
The key to success in the visual web is to have at least one highly relevant photo for each piece of content on your website. If you want people to share your products, content, reports, services, blog posts, content pages, articles or anything on your site (including your home page) you must have great images. Take an inventory of your website.

- Every page should have at least one relevant image.
  - o What images do you have to create?
  - o What images aren't good enough?
  - o Can you include multiple options (especially if your subject area is highly visual)?
- Images should be titled and tagged correctly.
  - o Images that are titled and tagged correctly have better visibility in search engines.
- Look at content from your competitors or in your industry that is generating pins or posts on Facebook.
  - o Do you have image content gaps on your website?
- Does sharable content have a unique web page?
  - o You may have content that people want to share that doesn't have a specific landing page or webpage. Sharing on sites like Pinterest and Facebook is dependent on sharing a link to a webpage.

The key is to take inventory of your website and make sure that any content that may be shared online has an attractive and relevant accompanying image.

5 IMAGES AND SOCIAL MEDIA

In addition to getting your website prepared for the visual web, make sure that your social media content is visual. Some brands think of Instagram and Pinterest as their "image sites" and focus Facebook and Twitter on content creation and development.

The reality is that all social media assets – blogs, Facebook, Twitter, LinkedIn, Google+ – are highly visual in terms of content that is viewed, interacted with and shared. The more visual content that you have for all of your social media assets, the more likely you are to be successful.

Consider:

- Images are the most shared content on Twitter.
- Images are the most clicked on content on Twitter.
- Images receive 50% more interactions on Facebook.
- Google+ users have uploaded 3.4 billion photos.[14]

- Recruiters spend more time examining a LinkedIn user's picture than actually reviewing the person's qualifications.[15]

All signs show us that any social media strategy must have great images to drive views, likes and interactions.

Images on Facebook

Look at the Facebook pages for some top brands. One of the things you'll notice is that they are almost exclusively posting images. Even posts that don't center around an image use an image as a focus point to grab attention and support the overall post. One of the things you'll notice in the Pampers Facebook Page (shot below) is that even the links that are shared focus on the image. This means that images on your site are vital to whether or not your content will be shared in social media, and how effective it will be if shared

The other thing you'll notice is that it isn't just about the image. The images posted are relevant to the brand and build the equity and positioning of the brand. Take RedBull for example. RedBull "gives you wings" and helps you achieve the extraordinary. It makes sense that their image strategy further promotes this by showing extreme sports.

Take a look at the Starbucks image strategy. They are showing beautiful images of their product in context. It isn't just about the picture but about how the picture paints a story.

One other thing you'll notice about the kinds of images that even big brands are sharing is that the images are not professionally produced. Many of them look as though average people with mobile phones took them. It used to be that getting "good photos" meant hiring a professional photographer to create professional and clean photos. With social media, we are learning that the kinds of photos that people actually want are real photos of real things taken by real people.

Images on Twitter

Twitter has also recently increased the focus that images play on their profile pages. As you can see in the screen shot, the top of the profile page now features an image front and center, similar to the cover image on Facebook. Additionally, on the left side of the profile page the images that have been Tweeted are featured. Twitter is increasing the prominence of images on the profile page because they know that it is the kind of content that people crave, and that drives connections with people, brands and businesses.

Images on LinkedIn

Even when sharing news and status updates on LinkedIn, we are seeing that images are playing a key role in driving attention to posts. You can see that the news that LinkedIn recommends has images front and center in drawing people into the content. Images are even taking prominence over the headlines by drawing people in and catching their eyes.

Even when scrolling through your newsfeed and looking at status updates from your friends, posts with images have more prominence than those without. Again, having a contextually relevant eye-catching photo is vital to success in getting views and traffic to your content.

In addition to status updates and top news, group discussions also heavily feature the image in any content or links that are posted. The reality is that if you want your content or news to be viewed, interacted with or clicked on in LinkedIn, you need great images.

Images in Google+

Even on Google+, images are highlighted in the newsfeed - both images associated with content linked to other places on the web, as well as images posted directly to Google+.

Again, images are featured in the newsfeed because they draw people to your content and drive people to engage with your content.

Images in Blog Posts

In the last chapter we covered images on your website; images for your blog posts are particularly important. In fact, articles and blog posts with images get 94% more total views than those without.[16]

But it isn't enough just to have a slightly relevant stock photo. If you want your content to travel effectively on Pinterest, Google+ and Facebook, a highly relevant image that brings the story to life is key.

Many people will say that your blog is the hub of your online marketing – it is the main source that you drive people to from social networks. If you want your blog content to travel to social media, you absolutely MUST have good images.

Social Media Image Checklist

As you can see, images and visual communication are vital to your success on all social networks – even those that aren't "image networks". The key takeaway of this section is to assess your existing social media accounts. Do you have the image content that people crave and that will help you be successful? Ask yourself:

- Are you posting images?
- Are they interesting and relevant?
- Do the images tell a story?
- Are your images gaining interactions?
- Are your images gaining shares/retweets/repins?
- Do you have an image strategy for each social network?

If you don't have great photos as a part of your existing social media strategy, you are missing out.

6 IMAGES ON SOCIAL MEDIA CASE STUDY: HUBSPOT AND PURE MICHIGAN GET IT RIGHT

HubSpot Harnesses Images to Drive Social Engagements and Generate Leads

HubSpot provides marketing software that helps companies attract leads and convert them into customers. A pioneer in inbound marketing, HubSpot aims to help its customers create marketing that people actually love. Since they are an online marketing company, it makes sense that they employ best practices in Visual Social Media Marketing and have seen considerable results with it.

HubSpot has been harnessing the power of images to drive views, engagements, clicks and leads across social media. Images are a key part of success in driving engagements on Facebook, blog posts, Twitter and Pinterest and are also driving targeted traffic back to HubSpot.com. HubSpot found that images are more successful at driving social engagement and traffic than text or link posts.

I caught up with Brittany Leaning, Social Media Manager at HubSpot, to learn about how images are transforming their social media content.

Facebook

HubSpot has seen a huge transformation in consumer appetite for images and the effectiveness of images on Facebook. On Facebook, images are paired with shortened links that drive people back to targeted content on HubSpot.com

Over the past year, HubSpot has shifted their strategy to include more images in the newsfeed. It used to be that about 75% of posts were text with links and now 75% of the posts are images. HubSpot takes social media very seriously and has specific lead generation objectives from their social media marketing.

If you'll take a look at HubSpot's Facebook page (www.facebook.com/HubSpot), you'll see that almost every single post contains an image – and the images are engaging and descriptive of the content. Using images on Facebook has driven results: a significant increase in leads from Facebook.

Why Are Images So Effective?

According to Brittany, when it comes to the Facebook newsfeed, brands are competing against lots of great content – cute pictures of kittens, babies, funny quotes and videos. In order to break through the noise, brands need to catch people's attention, and images that are engaging and interesting appear to be the best type of content to draw people in.

What Kinds of Images Does HubSpot Post?

HubSpot shares a variety of images across social networks. HubSpot has the ability to turn almost any content into an engaging image that is ready for sharing on their blog, Facebook, Twitter, Pinterest or any other social network.

One of the keys to success is variety – it isn't about posting the same image every day. People like variety, plus different content appeals to different people. Some of the types of images and content they share include:

eBook covers that drive people to download a free eBook:

These tend to be best at driving leads.

An image with a link to a blog post:

This is a great way to drive traffic to blog posts while engaging visually.

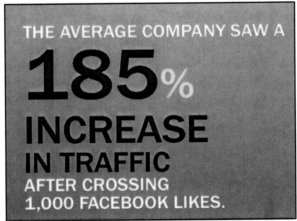

Stats on a slide:

Similar to fun facts – these engage people and are quick and easy to create.

A photo of text:

Don't forget to take actual photos or take photos of text to tell your story.

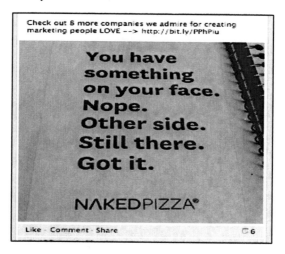

Inspiring quotes:

These tend to be popular on social media in general and can be effective if they link back to your business.

Cartoons:

They can be a lighthearted and fun way to share a message.

Would you rather:

One way to engage people is with a simple question that gets them thinking.

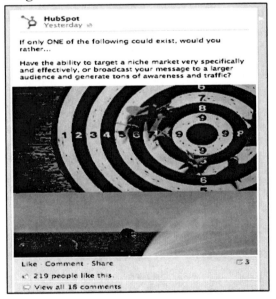

Provocative images:

These grab attention and encourage participation and sharing.

Funny animals:

Using these with a relevant message also capitalizes on the internet's love for cute animals.

Infographics:

Use these to share a data story visually.

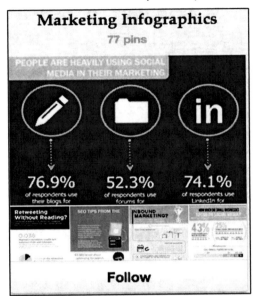

Customer testimonials:

These are a highly visual way to share successes.

Fun facts:

This is a lighthearted way to engage people in a way that is highly sharable.

Text on a slide:

This can be a fast and simple way to create a relevant and descriptive graphic.

Tips for success:
- ✓ Images that are descriptive of the content tend to be more effective. An image of a cover of an eBook is better at driving clicks to the eBook than perhaps a general image of what the eBook is about.
- ✓ Mix it up – don't post the same pictures every day.
- ✓ Post fun pictures to get people engaged – don't be too serious.
- ✓ Ask questions with your posts to get people commenting and participating.
- ✓ When it comes to blog posts, if a great post doesn't have an interesting and relevant image, it is less likely to be clicked on.
- ✓ Images should be contextually relevant to the content that they link to.
- ✓ If the image isn't directly connected to the content, include a blurb and ask a question that is relevant to the image as well as the blog post so that they are both connected.

Pure Michigan Uses Images to Gain Traction in Social Media

Chad Wiebesick, the Director of Social Media and Interactive Marketing for the Michigan Economic Development Corporation, uses images across social media to drive awareness and engagement.

Background

The goal of the Pure Michigan campaign is to drive tourism to the state of Michigan. The objective of social media marketing is to showcase how marvelous and magnificent Michigan can be and to drive people to work, play and vacation in the state. Pure Michigan has been successfully using social media marketing for some time now, but has found that recently images have played a bigger role in their success across channels.

Solution

Pure Michigan uses images across social networks to drive engagement and get fans involved in the brand. Since the Pure Michigan brand is highly visual, images are key to gaining traction.

"Our marketing channels are not Silos," said Wiebesick in a reflection about the role that content plays across social networks. Content from Facebook may be cross-populated or repositioned on a site like Pinterest.

Pure Michigan is posting images to all of their primary social networks including Facebook, Twitter, Pinterest and Google+.

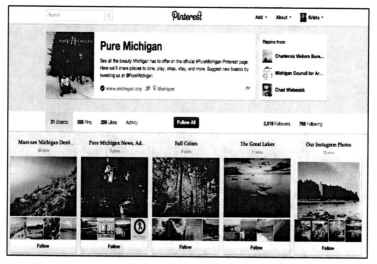

On Facebook, Pure Michigan shares a wide variety of images and sees their role partly as curators of a gallery of stunning images that bring the Pure Michigan brand to life. In addition to sharing images of stunning landscapes that look like they belong in National Geographic, they also share fun images that are culturally relevant.

In one instance a fan had posted an image of a cloud that looked like a Mitten (which is also the shape of Michigan's Lower Peninsula). Pure Michigan shared it on Facebook and it instantly received traction – with some fans even taking screenshots and reposting it on their own Facebook accounts.

In addition to just posting images, they try to make the page fun and engaging. Pure Michigan will post photos and ask fans to guess the location, have them caption a cartoon, or link it back to trivia.

Trying and experimenting with different photos is part of the key to success, and Pure Michigan shares everything from sweeping and majestic photos, to cartoons, to user generated content, to infographics.

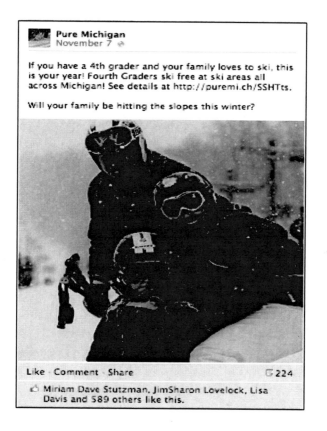

Pure Michigan
November 7

If you have a 4th grader and your family loves to ski, this is your year! Fourth Graders ski free at ski areas all across Michigan! See details at http://puremi.ch/SSHTts.

Will your family be hitting the slopes this winter?

Like · Comment · Share   224

Miriam Dave Stutzman, JimSharon Lovelock, Lisa Davis and 589 others like this.

Tip for Success:

✓ Don't just post photos, make them fun – with trivia, fill in the blanks, caption contests, or other simple and fun interactive opportunities.

✓ Images make great content across social networks – Like Facebook, Google+, Pinterest, and Twitter.

✓ Mix it up and try sharing different kinds of photos.

✓ User generated photos can also be a fun way to engage fans.

KRISTA NEHER

7 PINTEREST FOR BUSINESS

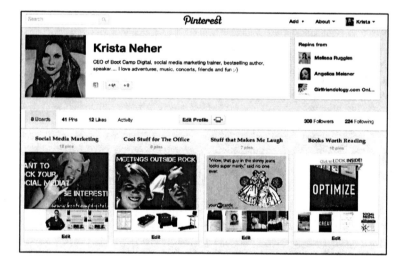

Pinterest is one of the key social media tools that is driving Visual Social Media Marketing, and in a big way it is what brought attention to the trend of the visual web. Pinterest is taking the social media world by storm; it is the fastest growing independent social network in the history of social media and it is highly visual. Both individuals and businesses are using Pinterest to share what they love and to build an audience around interesting content.

What is Pinterest and How Does it Work?

Pinterest is your "online pinboard" where "pinners" create boards based on a specific topic and "pin" individual pieces of content related to the board. So I may create a pinboard called "Social Media Infographics" where I share infographics about social media marketing, and another called "Cool Stuff for the Office" where I share the most interesting office accessories, and yet another called "Coffee Addiction" where I share coffee stuff.

Here are the basics of Pinterest:

- A person or business can have a Pinterest account. Pinterest offers verified accounts for businesses.
- A "pin" is an individual item or piece of content that is pinned or shared on Pinterest.
- A pinboard is a collection of pins, typically based around a specific topic.
- A Pinterest account or user can have an unlimited number of pinboards with an unlimited number of items pinned within each board.
- When a user logs in to Pinterest, he or she sees a newsfeed (similar to Facebook or LinkedIn) that shows recent pins from pinners that he or she follows.
- Pinterest is a social network – users can follow other people or just specific boards from other people. They can also like, repin and comment on pins posted by others.
- Pins are public, which means that you can search Pinterest to find things that interest you, and even people who don't follow you can find your pins.

- If you want a couple of private boards Pinterest has Secret Boards that only you and those you give permission to can see.

In the example below you can see my friend Lat's Pinterest account. She has a number of pin boards to represent the things that she finds interesting. When she finds a great recipe that she might want to make some day, she pins it to her Yummies board.

It serves as a place for her to share and keep track of the things she is interested in.

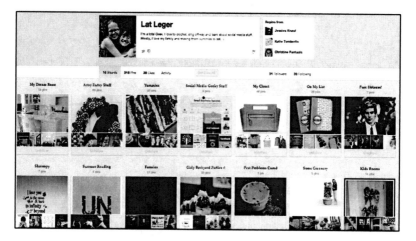

What is a Pin?
A "pin" is the item or content that is shared on Pinterest. The first thing you'll notice about pins is that they are highly visual. While you may be "Pinning" an article or website, Pinterest will pull the images from the site and use them as the focus of the content.

To pin content, select the add button from your Pinterest

account. You'll be prompted to either add a pin or upload a pin. Uploading a pin will prompt you to upload an image from your computer. If you choose this option, when people click on your pin they will only be brought to a larger version of the image you uploaded, not a website.

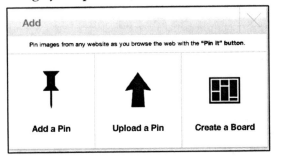

The other option is to add a pin, which prompts you to insert a URL or website address from the internet. The advantage of pinning content or images from your website (or another website) is that people can click-through to find the actual article or original website with the content.

In the next example, I'm pinning an article about Instagram from the Boot Camp Digital blog. Once I put the link into the input box, Pinterest will find the images that are on that webpage, and allow me to select the image that best represents my post.

The pin will then appear on my board and the people who follow me will see my latest pin appear in their newsfeed. As you can see, the pin is highly focused around the image. If the image isn't descriptive of the content, it is unlikely that people will be interested enough to click through and look at your content.

3 Tips for Getting Your Business on Instagram.... I LOVE Instagram photos!

bootcampdigital.com

If a page doesn't have an image, or if there are issues with the image, a blank space will appear where the image should be. Obviously, this isn't very engaging and it is unlikely that anyone will like, comment, repin or click on a pin without an image.

My latest column on Smart Business about why you might be missing the point of social media marketing.

sbnonline.com

In addition to the pin itself focusing around the image, the board (which is what people will see when they go to your Pinterest account) is centered around your images.

If you don't have great images on your website, your content won't travel well on Pinterest, and you will miss out on getting traffic from this growing social network.

Why Pinterest is Important for Businesses
Pinterest is important for a number of reasons. First, Pinterest is a large social network that is growing quickly. Second, it has highly engaged users.

- Pinterest buyers spend more money, more often than any of the other top 5 social media sites.[17]
- American consumers who use Pinterest follow an average of 9.3 retail companies on the network.[18]
- The number of daily Pinterest users has increased by 145% since January 2012.[19]

One of the main reasons that Pinterest is so powerful for businesses is that it sends massive amounts of traffic to other websites on the internet. Pinterest currently sends more traffic to other businesses than Google+, YouTube and LinkedIn combined[20]. When content is pinned or posted to Pinterest, people often click on it to find the original source of the pin, which sends the user to the website where the content is hosted. Pinterest is the #1 source of traffic to MarthaStewart.com.

For example, I might find a great home décor idea, and I want to see exactly how the room was put together and find more details, so I'll click on the image and go to the page on MarthaStewart.com with the article and image.

Pinners often click on images of products they like and actually buy. Studies show that pinners are 10% more likely to buy, compared to traffic from other social networks, and they spend 10% more on average.[21]

Additionally, Pinterest is a highly "viral" social network, which means that content on Pinterest can spread quickly. 80% of pins on Pinterest are repins[22], which means that Pinners like to share content that is already on the site. This means that sharing your content on Pinterest could mean that it gains views and repins quickly.

Pinterest is also great for businesses because it is public. You can search for pins, boards or users on almost any topic to see what people are pinning. On Pinterest you can follow anyone (they don't have to approve you like they do on Facebook) and anyone can follow you.

This means that Pinterest can be used for community building (finding and connecting with people who share your interest) or research. We use Pinterest to research visual content that people like and share. As you consider your image strategy, Pinterest should be a research stop for you.

Finding Content Pinned from Your Site
Another valuable exercise on Pinterest is to find content that has been pinned from your site. This will allow you to see what content on your site (and your competitors' sites) is naturally sharable.

Go to www.pinterest.com/source/yourdomain.com to see content pinned from any website.

How Businesses are Using Pinterest
In the next chapter you'll see some Pinterest case studies, but here are some of the strategic ways that businesses are using Pinterest:

- **Traffic** - To drive traffic to their website by pinning their content (blog posts with images, infographics, product pictures, etc).
- **Branding** - To bring their brand to life by creating boards that showcase what their brand stands for.
- **Awareness** - To build awareness by getting in front of the audiences they want to connect with.
- **Sales** – To increase direct sales as a result of their participation on Pinterest.
- **Community** – To build community and deepen connections with their audience by engaging and participating on Pinterest.
- **Resource** – To create a resource for press, employees, customers, etc. By creating pinboards with comprehensive information about a given topic, Pinterest can become a visual resource guide.
- **Research** – To understand the content that people share.

Pinterest Power Tips for Businesses

✓ Make sure that all of the content on your site is "pinable," meaning there is a relevant image to accompany each of the pages or products on your website.

✓ Add the "pin it" button to pages or content that is highly visual like product pages, infographics or blog posts.

✓ Create a Pinterest account and start pinning.

✓ Mix it up – don't strictly pin things from your own site – think about your audience and the community that they are in and ask yourself, "What is of interest to my audience?"

✓ Engage on Pinterest – like other social networks, you get out what you put in. To get noticed on Pinterest, businesses have to participate by liking, commenting on and repining other people's content.

✓ Consider your social media strategy – determine how Pinterest fits in with the rest of your social media marketing strategy.
✓ Connect Pinterest with your other online assets – link to it on your website and other social networks.

8 PINTEREST CASE STUDIES – SONY, PETPLAN, AND JETSETTER

Brands are using Pinterest in different ways. Assess your business goals and objectives, as well as the resources available, to determine the Pinterest approach that makes the most sense for you.

Sony Drives Traffic with Pinterest

Sony saw an opportunity to grow their brand using Pinterest. In 2012, they noticed that many of their customers and prospects were on Pinterest and were pinning content that was related to the Sony brand. Sony started by researching what people were already pinning and developed a strategy.

First, they clearly identified their goals for Pinterest:

1. Drive sales to the website.
2. Increase brand affinity.
3. Grow the Sony community.

Once they had their objectives, they spent *three months* researching social content that could work on Pinterest and building their initial boards.

Sony launched their Pinterest account with support both internally and externally. The account launched with an internal contest, which asked Sony employees to share what Sony means to them. This led to several hundred employee boards and content that Sony could repin to their account.

Sony focuses on having a mix of boards to appeal to brand fans, and they also create their own unique images just for Pinterest. Sony continues to see month-over-month increases in their traffic from Pinterest, and followers, likes and comments as their pins continue to grow.

Results:

- 800% increase in traffic from Pinterest.
- 10x the number of clicks on the Pin It button vs. the Tweet It button.
- Over 4 million brand impressions.
- Over 2,300 brand followers.
- 2.5x the traffic generated from Twitter.

Petplan Engages Pet Parents on Pinterest

Petplan is a pet insurance company that focuses on providing high quality content and exceptional customer service. Their objectives for joining Pinterest were to provide pet owners with tools to care for their pets, to attract new audiences through compelling and relevant content, and to establish brand leadership in the pet health space.

Petplan used Pinterest to visually communicate their expertise and share their brand personality. After researching trending topics on Pinterest as well as popular content from other online and offline channels, Petplan launched their Pinterest account which included images and educational content.

Petplan also wanted to increase awareness of the need for pet insurance as well as the availability. They added "Pin It" buttons to their site as well as their other online marketing outlets like email. They also optimized their on-site content for Pinterest. This attracted a new audience of pinners interested in their pets' health.

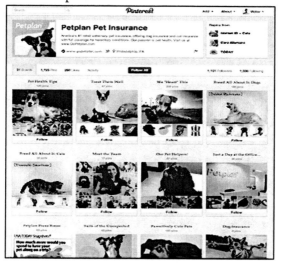

Results

Within only a few months, Pinterest became Petplan's second-highest source of social network referral traffic. Pinterest generates 69% more page views and 97% greater time on-site than Twitter.

"We saw great success in being able to attract people to our brand with general, broad-reaching content. Our success went beyond our direct community – two months after creating our Pinterest presence, *Social Media Delivered* included Petplan on its list of 'Top 20 Companies on Pinterest.'" – Natasha Ashton, CEO of Petplan.

Results:

- 87% increase in new site traffic.
- 35% increase in page views.
- 12.5% increase in insurance quote requests.

Their efforts on Pinterest have also led to success in search engine optimization.

"After less than nine months of building a Pinterest presence, a Google search for 'pet health tips' yields a Petplan pinboard within the first three results."[23]

Jetsetter Engages with Pinterest Contests

Jetsetter is a flash sale site for travel. They joined Pinterest to cultivate and engage their brand advocates, to empower the community to share their travel inspiration, and to obtain actionable feedback on their website. Jetsetter ran 3 different contests to engage their audience on Pinterest.

Curation Promotion

To achieve this, Jetsetter created a Curation promotion where they invited over a million of their members to create boards to reflect the most inspiring travel destinations based on images from Jetsetter.com. A panel of celebrity judges was tasked with selecting the winning boards.

During the contest, fans pinned over 50,000 images in under a month – Pinterest referral traffic increased 100% and page views on the website increased by 150%.

"When we unleashed our community to share their favorite Jetsetter content on Pinterest, it generated a ton of ideas for how to make our own Pinterest boards more compelling. We also learned which photos on our site resonate the most with our users, and it's since influenced our content strategy," said Jon Goldman, Social Media Manager for Jetsetter.

Pinterest Scavenger Hunt

Jetsetter also launched a contest called "Pin Your Way to Paradise" which led members on a scavenger hunt across the Jetsetter website. Over a 2 week period, members were given daily clues prompting them to pin the photos that best matched the description of each clue.

Jetsetter was able to observe how pinners navigated the website to find the images. The response to the contest led to over 800 boards and 16,000 pins.

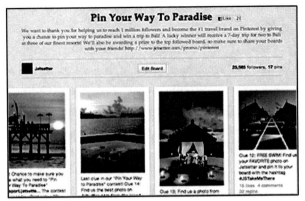

Group Boards Provide Collaboration

In another creative use of Pinterest, Jetsetter worked with a passionate fan to help him plan his vacation to Turks and Caicos. They collaboratively pinned ideas for the trip including what to bring, things to do, where to stay and more. They also crowd sourced tips and advice from other fans and experts, which allowed multiple people to contribute to the creation of a board that served a real purpose – to help someone plan a vacation.

The results were tremendous. The board had more than 720,000 Pinterest followers (5x more than Facebook and 20x more than Twitter) and users pinned over 9,500 times![24]

Top Brands on Pinterest

Looking for more Pinterest inspiration? Check out what top brands are doing on Pinterest for inspiration and best practices. Mashable named the top 8 brands on Pinterest:

1. Whole Foods
2. Martha Stewart
3. Better Homes and Gardens
4. Real Simple
5. West Elm
6. Bergdorf Goodman
7. Today
8. Travel Channel

I also recommend checking out:

- General Electric
- Home Depot
- Girlfriendology
- HubSpot
- Constant Contact

9 INSTAGRAM FOR BUSINESS

Instagram is quickly emerging as a social network to watch in social media. In 2012, Facebook purchased Instagram for $1 billion and the social network now has over 100 million users. Nearly 4 billion photos have been shared on Instagram since its launch, and 40% of brands have already adopted Instagram for marketing.[25]

Instagram isn't just worth watching because it is growing; it is worth watching because it underscores some trends in the evolution of social media. First, Instagram demonstrates the trend towards visual storytelling rather than just showing boring text. Second, Instagram highlights the trend towards visual documentation; users on Instagram and other social networks are visually documenting their experiences and their lives rather than writing about them.

While Instagram and other photo sites may come and go, these larger trends are fundamental behaviors that are exhibited across social networks.

What is Instagram and How Does it Work?

Instagram is a mobile application that allows users to take and share photos from their mobile phones. Instagram has two primary features. First, it allows users to edit their photos and create beautiful images. Second, it functions as a social network for image sharing.

Similar to most social networks, a user on Instagram can create a profile with basic information, and can follow other users, like images and leave comments. Unlike with other social networks, this all takes place through a mobile application and currently cannot be done on the web.

Instagram allows users to apply a number of "filters" to images that can take regular images and make them look extraordinary.

BEFORE   **AFTER**

As you can see above, Instagram allows average photos to become extraordinary, all with a few touches on a mobile phone. In addition to taking great photos, Instagram also allows users to share their photos in a number of different ways.

Images from Instagram can easily be shared on Facebook and Twitter. In addition, Instagram is a social network unto itself. On Instagram, users can view other users' photos (depending on privacy settings) and follow other users, as well as like and comment on images.

How Businesses are Using Instagram

Businesses use Instagram in a variety of ways. At present, there is no difference on Instagram between a personal account and a business account.

Create a Business Account – Take and Share Photos

Some businesses have corporate accounts on Instagram that they use to take and share images.

As the case studies in the next chapter will show you, it isn't enough to take photos and hope that your audience will magically build itself. Most of the brands that have been successful in building communities on Instagram spend time interacting with other users by following, commenting and liking photos. Using hashtags (covered in the next section) can also increase your awareness and reach on Instagram.

To begin using Instagram for a business, simply create a free account and begin taking photos with your mobile phone. Spend some time connecting with other users who are in your target audience to build your community.

Create a Business Account – Share Photos on Other Social Networks

Instagram can also be a quick and easy way to take photos to share on Facebook, Twitter, or other social networks. If you don't have time to invest in building a community on Instagram, consider using it as a way to create powerful image content.

Instagram Hashtags and Contests

Instagram can also be used to collect images around a specific topic. For example, I may ask people to use #VSMM when sharing pictures about this book, or when discussing Visual

Social Media Marketing. Since Instagram photos are searchable and public, I could see all of the images tagged with #VSMM and respond to them or share comments. In addition, anyone can simply search for #VSMM to see images shared with this hashtag.

Similar to Twitter, a hashtag is used as a part of a post to signify the theme of the image and make it searchable. Adding the "#" sign in front of a word or phrase makes it searchable. For example, I may tag a photo with #Cincinnati so that people who search for images of Cincinnati will see my photos.

Brands, businesses and celebrities are taking advantage of using hashtags on Instagram to both theme conversations and to run contests.

For example, Jason Mraz ran a contest asking Instagram users to translate his song "I Won't Give Up" into an image and tag it with #IWONTGIVEUP. A quick search on Instagram shows over 30,000 photos tagged with #IWONTGIVEUP that bring the song to life.

In addition to driving images shared on Instagram, the photo contest generated Tweets and Facebook posts from all types of people, including celebrities.

Randy Jackson ✓
@YO_RANDYJACKSON

🐦 Follow

Yo @jason_mraz #iwontgiveup
instagr.am/p/Guq6yWltTA/

8 Feb 12   ← Reply ⟲ Retweet ★
                      Favorite

Creating a hashtag for use on Instagram is as simple as choosing a phrase and checking that it isn't already in use. For example we chose #VSMM (Visual Social Media Marketing) for this book. There is no registration process for using a hashtag – simply choose something obvious that is not currently in use and spread the word. Publicizing the use of your hashtag is the key to success.

For example, Brooklyn Bowl created an Instagram contest where customers share photos tagged with #BrooklynBowl for a chance to win free tickets to a show. To date, over 5,400 photos have been uploaded to Instagram with #BrooklynBowl. One of the key advantages of encouraging Instagrammers to use your hashtag is that you bring your brand into the conversation.

For example, I may be bowling at Brooklyn Bowl and snapping photos of my friends to share on Facebook and Twitter. I would probably include a description of the photo but might not think to mention where the photo was taken. By adding the request to tag my photo with the venue #BrooklynBowl, Brooklyn Bowl is now a part of the discussion and is building awareness for their brand.

10 INSTAGRAM CASE STUDIES – *EASY TO ASSEMBLE*, PURE MICHIGAN, KOYAL WHOLESALE, AND DOGS OF INSTAGRAM

Case Study: *Easy to Assemble* Uses Instagram to Live-Stream their Premier on Facebook

Background

Easy to Assemble is a comedy that follows actress Illeana Douglas as she goes to work at IKEA in an attempt at a normal life. The show is aired live on the web and is sponsored by IKEA.

For the premier of the 4th season, social media manager Rick Yaeger knew that photos from behind the scenes of the premier would be a great way to drive engagement, build awareness and generate excitement from fans. Rick couldn't be at the premier himself, and he thought that the celebrity appeal of the cast might be a way to increase the appeal of the images taken at the event.

Rick also knew that if he required the cast to use a new tool, or to upload to more than one site, he wouldn't get a lot of participation. Fortunately, most of the cast was already using Instagram.

Rick turned to Instagram and a social media automation tool called IFTTT (If This Than That - www.ifttt.com) to create a live stream of stunning images on Facebook.

Action

Rick created a process using Instagram, IFTTT and Facebook to create a live stream on Facebook of photos taken by the cast from the premier. This created a great inventory of images for Facebook and other social networks, gave fans a look "behind the scenes" and built awareness and buzz for the premier.

The pitch to the cast members was simple: *since you will be taking pictures anyway, give me permission to follow you on Instagram, and anytime you take a photo during the Premier, I will automatically share it on Facebook and Twitter.*

During the premier, every time an Instagram photo was taken by a cast member, the image was automatically added to an album on Facebook and Tweeted. This created an almost live-stream of the event.

The effort of getting photos from the cast was successful because they didn't have to do anything that they were not already doing. Most of them already took and shared photos on Instagram – all they had to do was give access to allow their photos to be used on Facebook to promote the show.

Result

The result of this effort was that 32 images from the premier were uploaded onto the Facebook Page for *Easy To Assemble*, giving fans a behind the scenes look at the premier and the cast with essentially a Live Image Feed of the event. All of the photos have likes and views and many have comments.

This experiment allowed *Easy to Assemble* to test the concept of creating a real-time photo feed from Instagram to Facebook, which can be used in the future and promoted at other events.

Takeaways

Here are the key takeaways from how *Easy To Assemble* used Instagram:

- If you want people to do something, make it easy. Don't require them to upload to different places, etc.
- Use social networks that people are already using.
- Use automation to help social networks connect with one another.
- Social media content can be repurposed and posted to multiple sites – in this case Instagram, Facebook and Twitter.
- Behind the scenes and authentic photos are more sought after than standard stock photos or poses on the red carpet.

Case Study: Pure Michigan Becomes Visual Storytellers and Curators

Chad Wiebesick, the Director of Social Media and Interactive Marketing for the Michigan Economic Development Corporation, has been using Instagram to grow awareness for the Pure Michigan (#PureMichigan) brand since July of 2012.

Pure Michigan has successfully used Instagram to drive awareness, build followers and reach influencers.

The goal of the Pure Michigan campaign is to drive tourism to the state of Michigan.

Solution

Before Pure Michigan even had an Instagram account, fans picked up on the #PureMichgan hashtag from advertising campaigns and Twitter; they started taking photos on Instagram and tagging them with the #PureMichigan hashtag.

Upon recognizing this, Pure Michigan realized it was time to get on board and begin taking advantage of Instagram. They didn't just join Instagram, post photos and wait for people to take notice – they actively participated on Instagram by liking, commenting on and following other users.

They also encouraged Instagrammers to share their photos

with #PureMichigan for an opportunity to be featured on the Pure Michigan Instagram account. Featuring photos from fans allowed the fan to be the center of attention and get their "5 Minutes of Fame," which led to increased exposure for the Pure Michigan Instagram account.

In addition to featuring content from other users, Pure Michigan periodically chooses a big influencer on Instagram to become the official photographer for a weekend. With this promotion, they hand over the password to their account and allow one of their fans to be Pure Michigan for the weekend.

For the first test, Pure Michigan chose Instagram user TonyDetroit and gave him behind the scenes access to a NASCAR race held in Michigan. Tony was chosen because he had a large following on Instagram (300,000 followers) and took amazing photos.

He became the Instagram reporter for the event and shared behind the scenes pictures with Pure Michigan followers and his own. The fans loved it because they got to experience the event through the eyes of TonyDetroit, and his pictures were fabulous.

Results
Pure Michigan has over 9,700 followers and is one of the top Instagram accounts in the travel and tourism industry. The hashtag #PureMichigan has been used over 87,000 times and is growing at about 500 mentions a day. For perspective, this is more mentions than #Chrysler or #NationalGeographic.

Takeaways:

- **Like other users photos to get noticed** – Success on Instagram isn't just about posting content. Most brands have to work for their audience by participating.
- **Harness user generated content** – Asking your audience to participate is a great way to build traction and awareness within new audiences and communities. Make them the heroes by featuring their content.
- **Find influencers and use them to help grow your brand** – Every brand has influencers. Find the Influencers with audiences who are already talking about your brand and build relationships with them.
- **Connect to offline marketing** – Instagram and social media are great listening tools to see if your broader campaigns are gaining traction and can give you additional reach and awareness.

Koyal Wholesale Connects with Customers on Instagram

Background

Koyal Wholesale is the world's largest wedding and event supplies company with over 50,000 products shipping to more than 80 countries. Shreyans Parekh, who serves as Director of Marketing and Business Development, saw that a lot of iconic brands such as Starbucks and Nike had started utilizing Instagram and thought that it might be an opportunity to drive awareness and engagement for Koyal. Shreyans also saw Instagram as a useful mobile marketing tool, as he saw an uptick in orders and traffic coming from mobile and tablet devices through 2012.

Additionally, since the wedding and event industry is so visual, Instagram seemed like a great fit to get feedback on new products and showcase the newest and most interesting items in the catalog.

Koyal's Instagram account was created in December 2011 and now has over 4,000 followers with many photos getting hundreds of likes and comments.

Solution

Koyal joined Instagram and started by posting their product photos. They didn't get a very good response initially and it seemed as though they were talking to themselves.

They switched gears and started focusing on building community – interacting with event planners, florists, caterers and luxury hotels on Instagram to generate awareness for their account. They started using hashtags such as #weddingplanning, #eventplanning and #eventdecor to join conversations that others were searching for and began to find, follow, like and comment on other Instagrammers who were talking about weddings and events.

In addition, rather than focusing exclusively on wedding products, they posted lifestyle images, inspirational quotes and images from destination weddings.

Once they had built a base following, they resumed the effort to drive engagement with their content.

Koyal posted new products they discovered with calls to

action for their followers to **Like it or Leave it** or asking if it was **Hot or Not?** Once they started driving participation from their audience they received a lot of great feedback.

Koyal also created a Koyal Instagram Ambassador program. They searched Instagram and found the users that were posting and interacting with Koyal. Rather than searching for popular influencers, they looked for people who already liked the things they were posting. Koyal then created a program that incentivized these people to become ambassadors by giving them access to exclusive VIP discounts and product launches to inspire their Instagram community.

Interesting and engaging content was part of the key to success for Koyal. Some of the images they post on Instagram include:

- Wedding and event planners who are using their products in creative tablescapes or events.
- Quotes from event planners and industry leaders.
- **Hot or Not** and **Like it or Leave it** to engage fans in the process of choosing products.
- Hashtags like #WeddingWednesday to become the center of the wedding community on Instagram.
- Popular wedding destination photos.
- "Guess the location" images which drive engagement.

As you can see from their page, there is a lot of variety in the type of content posted.

Results

The ROI (Return on Investment) from Instagram is difficult to measure. Unlike Facebook, Pinterest or Twitter, Instagram doesn't allow for links to be included in comments or descriptions on the site, so traffic directly from Instagram can't be measured.

That being said, Instagram has shown measurable results in other ways. Posting contests on Instagram instantly doubled contest participants and has also driven awareness for new products.

In one instance, feedback from Instagram was actually used to improve a product in development by Koyal. An image of a cupcake stand with crystal trim was shared on Instagram with a request for feedback. Instagrammers commented that the crystal trim did not hang correctly and could obstruct the view of the cupcakes.

Koyal shared the feedback with their manufacturer overseas and released the final product to tremendous fanfare – with sneak peeks of the product launch on Instagram, of course. This helped Koyal to build a stronger market, sell a better product and demonstrate to their Instagram community that their feedback is truly valued.

Takeaways:

- People won't find your content organically; you have to find them.
- Interact and become a part of the community that you want to reach.
- Find interesting content to share from your own images, blogs, Pinterest and Instagram itself – anywhere that you find inspiration!
- Create pathways for interaction on Instagram.
- Connect and utilize Instagram with the rest of your social media platforms to create a comprehensive marketing mix.
- Identify and connect with your brand ambassadors on Instagram and foster the relationships through other channels as well.

Dogs of Instagram is Something to BARK About

Ahmed El Shourbagy started the DogsOfInstagram account in July of 2011; it quickly became one of the top accounts on Instagram with over 101,000 followers. He created the account to bring together the Dogs on Instagram because he realized that the humans of Instagram enjoyed sharing photos of their dogs. The hashtag #DogsOfInstagram has been used over 1.5 million times, and they recently broke a record with a single photo receiving nearly 22,000 likes and over 700 comments.

Background

Ahmed started DogsOfInstagram for personal enjoyment and as an experiment. He was a passionate Instagrammer and he wanted to see if he could build a brand on Instagram and generate interest around how man's best friend is present on the site.

What makes the DogsOfInstagram account interesting is that the images aren't taken by Ahmed – people on Instagram submit photos of their dogs and the cutest canines with the best photos are featured on the DogsOfInstagram account.

Once the account was created, it quickly gained traction, garnering hundreds of submissions every day. In order to have their image featured on the DogsOfInstagram account, submissions had to sign a release allowing the image to be re-uploaded to prevent any legal issues.

The account is a fun way for people to share their dog photos and get featured to the over 101,000 people who follow the DogsOfInstagram feed.

Solution

DogsOfInstagram is an amazing case study in building community and a following on Instagram.

Each day DogsOfInstagram features 2-3 new photos. Each photo on Instagram typically gets 100 – 150 comments, which is more than many national brands are getting on Facebook.

Ashley Paguyo saw the account and thought that there might be an opportunity to do something with it. She reached out to Ahmed and they started a Movember Dogs of Instagram campaign. "Movember" is a movement to raise awareness and funds to support prostate cancer by growing moustaches. For Movember, DogsOfInstagram asked people to send in moustache photos of their dogs.

How Did You Build the Instagram Following?

Like any social network, it isn't as simple as "if you build it, they will come". Building a following takes work, time and effort. In order to build traction and gain attention on Instagram, Ahmed spent time building a community and connecting with other Instagram users.

DogsOfInstagram gained traction by:

- Following people who shared photos of their dogs (Instagram's search option helped DogsOfInstagram to find these photos).
- Commenting on and liking dog pictures taken by other Instagrammers to build awareness for their account and to support other Instagrammers interested in dogs and photos of dogs.
- Asking people to share their photo (which dog owners loved).
- Tagging the pictures with the person who submitted the photo and including a comment to make the post more personal.
- Engaging the community made a difference; once people saw the page, they wanted to get their dog featured so they followed the account.
- Spreading through word of mouth – the more they promoted the community and members, the more the community promoted DogsOfInstagram.
- Tagging photos for search with terms like #dogsofinstagram #dog #breed etc to increase the searchability and discoverability of the images.

Additionally, on most social networks like Instagram, success leads to more success. As the DogsOfInstagram account became more popular, the images were often picked up and featured on the Instagram homepage. This led to more views, traffic and traction.

11 INFOGRAPHICS

Infographics have emerged as a popular Visual Social Media Marketing tool. An infographic is a visual way to share data or information. The idea is that by using graphics, information can be shared quickly because people can easily interpret and understand patterns and trends if it's explained visually.

Infographics have gained popularity over the past few years as a way to communicate information on social networks.

Infographics are typically longer-format images that tell a story and share information. My company, Boot Camp Digital, uses infographics heavily to share complex information and to tell stories visually, and we've had a ton of success. Our busiest day of all-time on our blog was Monday, October 29th, 2012 – the day we posted a "Cats in Social Media" infographic in honor of National Cat Day.
Our first infographic, Cincinnati Is Social, can be seen below.

Why Businesses Use Infographics

Businesses use infographics for a variety of reasons that are a strategic part of their overall social media marketing plan. The reason that infographics provide so much value for businesses is that people online like to share them, write about them and click on them, which means that they can drive traffic, branding, link-building, sales, exposure and social content for your brand.

In an interview with Avalaunch Media, a company that specializes in infographics (see more in the Case Study in the next chapter), we discussed the primary benefits of creating infographics:

- **Traffic** – First and foremost, infographics are a great way to drive traffic to a website. People love looking at infographics, so they often send large amounts of traffic to websites. *A strong promotion plan is needed to ensure that your infographic will generate traffic to your site.*
- **Branding** – Infographics can be good at positioning brands and building their equity. They are a great way to build your brand and associate it with a specific topic.
- **Link-Building** – One of the best ways to improve your SEO (search engine optimization) and get your company to the top of search engine results is to have other companies link to you. Since news sites and blogs often share infographics and include a link back to the company who created them, they can be a very powerful way to grow more links to your website.
- **Direct Sales** – In some instances, infographics can directly drive sales to a business. Especially in the B-to-B space, exposing your industry to thought leadership and new ideas through an infographic can generate sales.
- **Exposure** – Infographics drive exposure to brands and can build general awareness. Infographics are often picked up by niche blogs and news sites, and some infographics even gain attention in the national media.
- **Social Content** – Infographics are great social content and can generate likes, shares, +1s and more across social channels.

Most infographics will have multiple benefits and generate some level of traffic, branding, link-building, sales and exposure.

Process for Creating Infographics
The process of creating an infographic can be as simple or complex as is necessary to achieve your objectives. Regardless, here are the basic steps for creating infographics:

1. **Define the Concept** – the first step is to define the overall concept or premise of the infographic. What is the story that you want to tell, or the theme for the infographic? This may require research and creativity. Look for trending topics in your industry or interesting things that people aren't really talking about yet. For example, at Boot Camp Digital, we created an infographic called "Social Media vs. Hygiene" after we noticed the popularity of Tweets comparing social media adoption to hygiene.

2. **Research and Find Data Points** – Once a theme or general premise is determined, research, research, research. Some businesses will do primary research and conduct their own surveys; however, there is usually significant data already out there. Research the data on your topic – and you may have to get creative here.

3. **Build the Story** – Once you have data, begin mapping out the story that you want the data to tell. How does the data fit together to form a story. How can the data be displayed creatively? For example, we knew through research how many people check Facebook every day, so we researched the number of people that shower every day to create an interesting comparison. This may take some time, and you may

re-enter the research stage as you find data gaps in your story.

4. **Display it Visually** – After the story and supporting data are clear, begin the display of the infographic. This stage isn't just about creating a picture of the data – it is about using visuals to make the data more obvious or easier to understand. The goal of the design stage is to display the data in a way that supports the overall story or message. This may also be a complicated process with a number of rounds of revisions.

5. **Build a Promotion Plan** – Creating a great infographic is only half the battle – promoting it is the other half. Create a clear promotion plan for your infographic. Consider how you will use your social networks and your relationships with bloggers or press, as well as sponsored media, to get traction from your infographic. The key to promotion is getting the infographic in front of the right audiences on social networks and on news sites or blogs to get people talking. Plan your promotion upfront.

6. **Launch!** – Launch your infographic and execute your promotion plan. Be prepared to roll up your sleeves to spread the word.

As you consider your options for executing your infographic, you may be choosing between a DIY model or hiring somebody. At Boot Camp Digital, we primarily use a DIY model. We use a tool called Piktochart that has drag and drop software that helps us design the infographics. This costs about $15/month (www.Piktochart.com) and may be quicker, but probably less effective compared to hiring a designer.

Hiring a designer is also an option for executing your infographic. Designers may charge between $500 and $3,000 to create an infographic, depending on the organization, size, and complexity of the project. Hiring a designer will give you a completely customized infographic that is tailor-made for you.

Finally, a business may choose to hire an infographic firm to manage the entire infographic creation process. Firms like Avalaunch Media (www.AvalaunchMedia.com) can handle the entire process from inception to promotion of an infographic. These full-service infographic firms typically charge between $4k and $7k to create an infographic.

12 INFOGRAPHIC CASE STUDIES – AVALAUNCH MEDIA AND UNMETRIC SEE SUCCESS WITH INFOGRAPHICS

Avalaunch Media Drives Results with Infographics

Avalaunch Media has been in the online space since 2005 and has been creating infographics for the past 5 years (before infographics were even called infographics). Avalaunch even has an official "Infographic Launcher" as a part of their team.

Avalaunch helps companies harness infographics from the initial ideation stage all the way through to the promotion. They have experience in launching countless infographics across multiple industries. I met with Andrew Melchior to learn about how Avalaunch has successfully launched infographics for their clients.

Infographic Process

When a client signs up for an infographic, the first step is to do a creative brainstorm to generate the concept or angle for the infographic. The brainstorm starts with understanding the client goals and objectives.

The key to success in the brainstorming is to define clearly the objectives and strategy up front. Most businesses don't have a clear idea as to why they are creating an infographic or what they want to achieve from it. The strategy should be defined before the brainstorm begins so that ideas can be effectively evaluated.

The brainstorm evolves around the concept for the infographic. For example, if a ski resort in Utah is looking for an infographic, it might want to strategically showcase why skiing is better in Utah. The brainstorm would generate concept ideas like the history of skiing, snowfall, weather related information, etc. Once a variety of concepts is created they will be evaluated vs. the objectives.

Upon selecting a concept, the next step is conducting research to determine what information is available. Proprietary or fresh new data always adds value. The process is to research, compile and refine until the data tells a compelling story.

Once the data and story are clear, the next step is the creative design phase, where the designer and the client work together to best visualize the story.

Promotion of Infographics
Creating a great infographic is only the first step towards infographic success. A great infographic won't deliver results if there isn't a clear plan for promotion.

Some of the items that should be in your infographic marketing toolbox include:

- **A network of relationships** including people, bloggers and news sites that can share and promote your infographic. Having a network of people that you can ask to help will ensure that your infographic gains traction early on.
- **Use your assets** to help spread the word. Facebook, newsletters, websites, LinkedIn, Pinterest, Twitter and other social networks are all great ways to share your infographic with your existing customers and fans.
- **Pump it up with earned channels or ads.** Avalaunch normally pushes graphics out through its earned/owned channels and hopes to see traction. If the infographic doesn't get traction organically, promoted channels can help drive initial views.

Common Mistakes

Some of the most common mistakes that Andrew sees are:

- Overbranding – the data and information should be the message, not the brand creating it.
- Matching brand style guides making it look like an ad, not an interesting piece of content.
- Trying to sell when it doesn't fit by inserting "buy now" buttons throughout an infographic.
- Choosing an unoriginal topic.

Interestingness and Good Content for the Infographic is Key

The most important thing is that you create an infographic that is interesting. Here are some tips to hone in on socially interesting content for infographics:

- Research ideas on social media to see what people are already talking about related to your industry.
- Look at the top shared content in your industry and outside of your industry to understand what types of things are popular.
- Pay attention to what is trending on Twitter, Reddit, YouTube, Digg, humor sites, How Stuff Works, etc to get ideas and inspiration.
- Use different keyword phrases and search a variety of social media and news sites for inspiration.

Example: Pinnable Business

Pinnablebusiness.com wanted to become an authority on Pinterest, so Avalaunch created an infographic for them to showcase their research and knowledge on Pinterest.

The infographic was posted on Mashable immediately and received over 5,000 shares across Facebook, Twitter and Pinterest. The infographic also sent tens of thousands of visitors to pinnablebusiness.com over several days and the overall site traffic went from double digits to five digits overnight.

Unmetric Drives Sales and Awareness with Infographics

Unmetric is a social media benchmarking company that monitors the daily activity on the social media outposts of brands to analyze competitors and benchmark performance. I had the opportunity to speak with Peter Claridge, the Manager of Global Marketing, who shared how Unmetric has used infographics to drive awareness and generate sales.

Background

Since Unmetric has access to unique industry data, they decided that infographics and visually displaying information would be a key strategy for online. Unmetric was defining a new category in the area of social media intelligence - it needed an interesting way to break through and get noticed in the industry.

Solution

Unmetric launched its first infographic in June 2012 as a test to see if infographics could help it achieve their objectives of building awareness for social media intelligence in the marketing and advertising communities. Its first infographic about the NBA (National Basketball Association) was picked up by ESPN and published in AdWeek, so executives knew they were onto something.

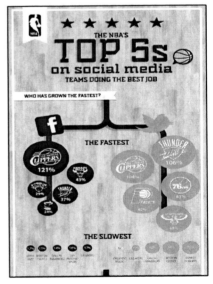

The strategy has evolved to target specific industries that have business development opportunities, such as the luxury brand or fast food industry. This has led to a clear and measurable number of leads, sales and business results.

Results

Unmetric has seen tremendous results from its infographics including generating awareness and driving sales.

Unmetric also received significant media attention from its infographics. It has had infographics posted on news sites like Mashable, ESPN and AdWeek. In addition, the infographics have been picked up by niche news sites, which increases its reach within the verticals it targets.

The real results are in the leads, sales and inquiries that have been generated from infographics. When Unmetric launched the Luxury Marketing infographics, it received inquiries from multiple marketing offices of an iconic luxury clothing brand company that will likely become a client. It also received 8 – 10 inquiries from other luxury brands asking why they weren't included in the infographics.

One of its newer clients, a global energy supply company, originally heard about Unmetric through their infographics. Coca-Cola mentioned data from an Unmetric infographic in its Q3 earnings report as a way to justify its investment in sponsoring the Olympics.

Infographics have been extremely powerful in generating leads with brands calling Unmetric instead of Unmetric having to knock on doors.

Takeaways

- **Don't just make an infographic, link it back to your strategy** – many businesses hear the buzz about infographics and jump in and start creating something. Think about your business objectives and link the content of your infographic back to your goals and target audience.
- **Even if you have great infographics, you need a strong promotion plan** – just creating an infographic, and having a PR team doesn't guarantee that the infographic will be successful. Have a promotion plan and build relationships with people who can help promote the infographic.

You can see parts of Unmetric's popular infographics below - the complete infographics are too long to include. You can see the complete infographics at http://blog.unmetric.com/category/infographics/

13 IMAGES TO CREATE FOR THE VISUAL WEB

We have now covered why images are valuable for your online presence, reviewed the key image social networks Instagram and Pinterest and covered one of the most popular types of social images – Infographics.

A big part of success in using images online is to be creative in using different types of images to drive your brand online. This chapter will give you inspiration and ideas for the types of images that you can create to harness the power of the visual web.

POWERTIP: Include your brand or website as a watermark on the bottom of your images to drive traffic and awareness for your business.

Stock Photo Plus Words

Stock photos can be found on sites like istockphoto, fotolia or sxc.hu and text can be added in most photo editing software.

Real Images Plus Words

In addition to using stock photos, any images can be used as a part of a screenshot with text added. For example, to create the image below I took a photo on Instagram and uploaded it to my computer. Next, I put the image into Microsoft word, where I simply added text on top of it using text boxes. To create the final image, I simply took a screenshot of the picture with the text on top.

Images to Show the Steps to Do Something

These images can be created simply by taking multiple photos and editing them together into a single image.

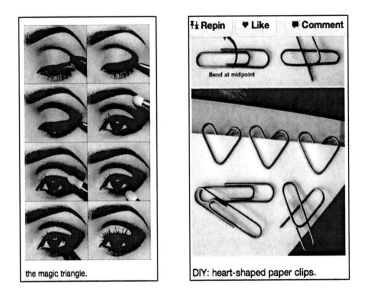

the magic triangle.

Repin   **Like**   **Comment**

Bend at midpoint

DIY: heart-shaped paper clips.

Photo of Words

Photos of words can easily be created in PowerPoint or even in a word document.

WHEN a NEW DAY BEGINS, SMILE GRATEFULLY.

STEVE MARABOLI

Girlfriendology.com

Girlfriendology
Liked · October 4 via HootSuite

"When a new day begins, smile gratefully."
Steve Maraboli: #quote http://ow.ly/aOR4P

Like · Comment · Share

Valerie Macarie and 93 others like this.

48 shares

Write a comment...

Sponsored   Create an Ad

Kevin Flynn likes Jeff Cramerding for Hamilton County Treasurer

Jeff Cramerding for Hamilton County Treasurer
Like

Create a Relevant Graphic
Custom graphics can be created by a designer to illustrate key points.

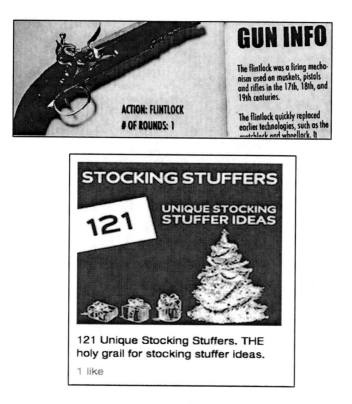

Use a Tool to Create an Image

For example, SomeECards images are often used on social media.

Draw Something and Snap A Picture

Not comfortable with Photoshop? Try drawing something and taking a photo for a quick way to get a great sharable image.

Design a Mini-Infographic
To get a single point across, try creating a mini infographic.

Photos of Real Things
Taking photos of real things is easy – and you can use Instagram to make them extra fabulous.

Holiday Nails

Candy Cane Place Card Holders

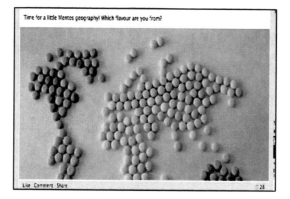

KRISTA NEHER

14 YOUR ACTION PLAN FOR VISUAL SOCIAL MEDIA MARKETING #VSMM

Now that you've completed the book, the next step is to take action! This is where you put what you've learned into action to get real results for your business. These checklists will help you get started!

For a downloadable version of these checklists, go to www.VisualSocialMediaMarketing.com

Visual Marketing is the key to unlocking success in the web – take the time to build a clear image strategy to take advantage of this quickly growing trend.

Thank you for joining me on this journey, and best of luck with your Visual Social Media Marketing #VSMM

On-Site Optimization

Optimize your site to encourage people to pin your content.

☐ Add <u>relevant</u> images to every page of your site.

- ☐ Make sure that everything you want people to share (your products, reports, blog posts, etc) has a relevant image attached to it.
- ☐ Think of how images can tell your story.
- ☐ Go to

  www.pinterest.com/source/yourdomainname.com to see what content people are already pinning from your site and your competitors' sites.
- ☐ Build a strategy to create visual content for all social networks.
  - o Facebook
  - o Twitter
  - o Pinterest
  - o Blog Posts

TYPES OF IMAGES

Be sure that you have a library of relevant images to use across social media and on your website.

- ☐ Infographics
  - o Consider Piktochart.com as a tool to build your own infographics
- ☐ Stock Photos (with text to describe the content)
  - o SXC.hu (free) or Fotolia.com (paid)
- ☐ Text images (eg. powerpoint screenshots)

- ☐ Photos of hand-drawn illustrations or words
- ☐ Create descriptive photos (how-to images)
- ☐ Take images of real things
- ☐ Use words on a PowerPoint slide
- ☐ Create mini-infographics
- ☐ Cartoons
- ☐ Testimonials/Reviews as images
- ☐ Stats or fun facts as images
- ☐ Quote images
- ☐ User-generated images (images taken by others)
- ☐ Product images
- ☐ Add text to your photos
  - ○ Desktop photo editors, Phonto (photo app), Pixlr (online editor), PowerPoint, and screen capture.

PINTEREST CHECKLIST

Before getting started, be sure that you have a strategy and know who you want to reach. Understanding what you want to achieve and with whom you want to connect is the key to your success on Pinterest.

Pinterest Profile

- ☐ You can start by linking to your Facebook or Twitter account, or by creating a new stand-alone account.
- ☐ Create an obvious username and complete your information.

- o Use a relevant profile photo.
- o Verify your account as a business account.
- ☐ Create 8 – 10 boards.
    - o Board names should be as specific as possible.
    - o Keep board names short so that they can be fully displayed.
- ☐ Pin a minimum of 5 pieces of content to each board for completeness.

Growing Your Following

Remember that the more you give, the more you get – take the time to connect with the community!

- ☐ Follow others with similar interests.
- ☐ Comment on and like content.
- ☐ Repin from others with similar interests.
- ☐ Promote your Pinterest account on your website.
    - o Also promote on other social networks, email and through other existing communication channels.
- ☐ Post regularly to maximize your following.

INSTAGRAM CHECKLIST

Create an Instagram Account

- ☐ Set up an account (must be done from a smartphone).
    - o HINT: Use a consistent username.
- ☐ Take photos that relate to your business.
    - o Posting 3 – 5 times a week on Instagram is more than sufficient.
- ☐ Connect with the Instagram community.
    - o Follow and interact with other users (follow, comment and like).
    - o Participate in hashtags.
    - o Find your audience and similar accounts with which to engage.

Grow Your Business with Instagram

- ☐ Create a hashtag to be used when referencing your business.
    - o This will grow your brand awareness.
    - o Choose a hashtag that is simple, obvious, intuitive and easy to spell.
- ☐ Run a contest to encourage people to share their photos on Instagram with your hashtag.

☐ Promote your hashtag at the most relevant touch points with:

- o Employees
- o Customers
- o Partners

Encourage all of them to build your library for you!!!!

Instagram is a source for beautifully stunning images for your website, Facebook page, Twitter account and Pinterest. It isn't just a social network – it is a source for images for your social media strategy across sites. *

ABOUT THE AUTHOR

Krista Neher is the CEO of Boot Camp Digital, a Social Media and Internet Marketing Training company. She is also the author of the bestselling Social Media Field Guide and coauthor of the textbook Social Media Marketing: A Strategic Approach.

Krista is an international speaker and trainer, and has worked with companies in America, Europe, South America and Asia. She is a dedicated social media educator and created one of the first accredited Social Media Certification programs.

Krista has been involved in social media marketing for over 5 years and has worked with companies like P&G, GE, General Mills, The United States Senate, Remax, Macy's and many more.

Krista has also been a featured expert on leading news sites including CNN, Wired, The New York Times, CBS, NBC, Fox, Mashable and The Associated Press.

Sources:

[1] Roost http://blog.roost.com/featured-posts/roost-finds-photos-generate-50-more-impressions-on-facebook-pages-than-any-other-type-of-content/

[2] Bitrebels http://www.bitrebels.com/social/facebook-photos-the-astonishing-stats-infographic/

[3] DanZarrella http://danzarrella.com/infographic-how-to-get-more-likes-comments-and-shares-on-facebook.html#

[4] Appolocious http://www.appolicious.com/articles/8583-flipboard-named-apples-best-ipad-app-of-2010-gets-better-with-update

[5] Jeff Bullas http://www.jeffbullas.com/2012/01/03/6-social-media-networks-to-watch-in-2012-plus-infographics/

[6] Mashable http://mashable.com/2012/09/11/instagram-100-million/

[7] Digital Buzz Blog http://www.digitalbuzzblog.com/infographic-instagram-stats/

[8] http://prweek.tumblr.com/post/35068717700/instagram-hurricane-sandys-aftermath-as-sandy

[9] Emarketer http://www.emarketer.com/Article.aspx?R=1009320&ecid=a6506033675d47f881651943c21c5ed4

[10] HubSpot http://blog.HubSpot.com/blog/tabid/6307/bid/33423/19-Reasons-You-Should-Include-Visual-Content-in-Your-Marketing-Data.aspx#ixzz2BO1mXdOm

[11] Customer Magnetism http://www.customermagnetism.com/infographics/what-is-an-infographic/

[12] 3M Corporation http://www.billiondollargraphics.com/infographics.html

[13] Web Marketing Group http://www.webmarketinggroup.co.uk/Blog/why-every-seo-strategy-needs-infographics-1764.aspx

[14] http://insidegplus.com/2011/11/google-plus-statistics-

versus-facebook/

[15] http://www.businessinsider.com/common-linkedin-mistakes-2012-8?op=1

[16] http://www.jeffbullas.com/2012/05/28/6-powerful-reasons-why-you-should-include-images-in-your-marketing-infographic/

[17] http://www.marketingpilgrim.com/2012/11/sponsor-12-statistics-that-make-the-business-case-for-pinterest.html

[18] http://www.marketingpilgrim.com/2012/11/sponsor-12-statistics-that-make-the-business-case-for-pinterest.html

[19] http://www.marketingpilgrim.com/2012/11/sponsor-12-statistics-that-make-the-business-case-for-pinterest.html

[20] http://mashable.com/2012/02/01/pinterest-traffic-study/

[21] http://thesocialskinny.com/99-new-social-media-stats-for-2012/

[22] http://mashable.com/2012/03/12/pinterest-most-popular-categories-boards/

[23] http://business.pinterest.com/case-study-petplan/

[24] http://business.pinterest.com/case-study-jetsetter/

[25] http://www.huffingtonpost.com/brian-honigman/100-fascinating-social-me_b_2185281.html